Life Lessons

from THE INSPIRED WORD of GOD

BOOK of PSALMS

MAX LUCADO
General Editor

TABLE OF CONTENTS

HOW TO STUDY THE BIBLE

BY MAX LUCADO

*T*his is a peculiar book you are hold-ing. Words crafted in another lan-guage. Deeds done in a distant era. Events recorded in a far-off land. Counsel offered to a foreign people. This is a peculiar book.

It's surprising that anyone reads it. It's too old. Some of its writings date back five thousand years. It's too bizarre. The book speaks of incredible floods, fires, earth-quakes, and people with supernatural abilities. It's too radical. The Bible calls for undying devotion to a carpenter who called himself God's Son.

Logic says this book shouldn't survive. Too old, too bizarre, too radical.

The Bible has been banned, burned, scoffed, and ridiculed. Scholars have mocked it as foolish. Kings have branded it as illegal. A thousand times over it the grave has been dug and the dirge has begun, but somehow the Bible never stays in the grave. Not only has it survived, it has thrived. It is the single most popular book in all of his-tory. It has been the best-selling book in the world for years!

There is no way on earth to explain it. Which perhaps is the only explanation. The answer? The Bible's durability is not found on earth; it is found in heaven. For the millions who have tested its claims and claimed its promises, there is but one answer—the Bible is God's book and God's voice.

As you read it, you would be wise to give some thought to two questions. What is the purpose of the Bible? and How do I study the Bible? Time spent reflecting on these two issues will greatly enhance your Bible study.

What is the purpose of the Bible?

Let the Bible itself answer that question.

Since you were a child you have known the Holy Scriptures which are able to make you wise. And that wisdom leads to salvation through faith in Christ Jesus.

(2 Tim. 3:15)

The purpose of the Bible? Salvation. God's highest passion is to get his children home. His book, the Bible, describes his plan of salvation. The purpose of the Bible is to proclaim God's plan and passion to save his children.

That is the reason this book has endured through the centuries. It dares to tackle the toughest questions about life: Where do I go after I die? Is there a God? What do I do with my fears? The Bible offers answers to these crucial questions. It is the treasure map that leads us to God's highest treasure, eternal life.

But how do we use the Bible? Countless copies of Scripture sit unread on bookshelves and nightstands simply because people don't know how to read it. What can we do to make the Bible real in our lives?

The clearest answer is found in the words of Jesus.

"Ask," he promised, *"and God will give it to you. Search and you will find. Knock, and the door will open for you."*

(Matt. 7:7)

The first step in understanding the Bible is asking God to help us. We should read prayerfully. If anyone understands God's Word, it is because of God and not the reader.

But the Helper will teach you everything and will cause you to remember all that I told you. The Helper is the Holy Spirit whom the Father will send in my name.

(John 14:24)

Before reading the Bible, pray. Invite God to speak to you. Don't go to Scripture looking for your idea, go searching for his.

Not only should we read the Bible prayerfully, we should read it carefully. *Search and you will find* is the pledge. The Bible is not a newspaper to be skimmed but rather a mine to be quarried. *Search for it like silver, and hunt for it like hidden treasure. Then you will understand respect for the LORD, and you will find that you know God* (Prov. 2:4).

Any worthy find requires effort. The Bible is no exception. To understand the Bible you don't have to be brilliant, but you must be willing to roll up your sleeves and search.

Be a worker who is not ashamed and who uses the true teaching in the right way.

(2 Tim. 2:15)

Here's a practical point. Study the Bible a bit at a time. Hunger is not satisfied by eating twenty-one meals in one sitting once a week. The body needs a steady diet to remain strong. So does the soul. When God sent food to his people in the wilderness, he didn't provide loaves already made. Instead, he sent them manna in the shape of *thin flakes, like frost . . . on the desert ground* (Exod. 16:14).

God gave manna in limited portions.

God sends spiritual food the same way. He opens the heavens with just enough nutrients for today's hunger. He provides, *a command here, a command there. A rule here, a rule there. A little lesson here, a little lesson there* (Isa. 28:10).

Don't be discouraged if your reading reaps a small harvest. Some days a lesser portion is all that is needed. What is important is to search every day for that day's message. A steady diet of God's Word over a lifetime builds a healthy soul and mind.

A little girl returned from her first day at school. Her mom asked, "Did you learn anything?" "Apparently not enough," the girl responded, "I have to go back tomorrow and the next day and the next. . . ."

Such is the case with learning. And such is the case with Bible study. Understanding comes little by little over a lifetime.

There is a third step in understanding the Bible. After the asking and seeking comes the knocking. After you ask and search, then knock.

Knock, and the door will open for you.
(Matt. 7:7)

To knock is to stand at God's door. To make yourself available. To climb the steps, cross the porch, stand at the doorway, and

volunteer. Knocking goes beyond the realm of thinking and into the realm of acting.

To knock is to ask, What can I do? How can I obey? Where can I go?

It's one thing to know what to do. It's another to do it. But for those who do it, those who choose to obey, a special reward awaits them.

The truly happy are those who carefully study God's perfect law that makes people free, and they continue to study it. They do not forget what they heard, but they obey what God's teaching says. Those who do this will be made happy.
(James 1:25)

What a promise. Happiness comes to those who do what they read! It's the same with medicine. If you only read the label but ignore the pills, it won't help. It's the same with food. If you only read the recipe but never cook, you won't be fed. And it's the same with the Bible. If you only read the words but never obey, you'll never know the joy God has promised.

Ask. Search. Knock. Simple, isn't it? Why don't you give it a try? If you do, you'll see why you are holding the most remarkable book in history.

PSALMS

INTRODUCTION

Worship. In two thousand years we haven't worked out the kinks. We still struggle for the right words in prayer. We still fumble over Scripture. We don't know when to kneel. We don't know when we stand. We don't know how to pray.

Worship is a daunting task.

For that reason, God gave us the Psalms— a praisebook for God's people. The Psalms could be titled *God's Book of Common Prayer*. This collection of hymns and petitions are strung together by one thread—a heart hungry for God.

Some are defiant. Others are reverent. Some are to be sung. Others are to be prayed. Some are intensely personal. Others are written as if the whole world would use them. Some were penned in caves, others in temples.

But all have one purpose—to give us the words to say when we stand before God.

The very variety should remind us that worship is personal. No secret formula exists. What moves you may stymie another. Each worships differently. But each should worship.

This book will help you do just that.

Here is a hint. Don't just read the prayers of these saints, pray them. Experience their energy. Imitate their honesty. Enjoy their creativity. Let these souls lead you in worship.

And let's remember. The language of worship is not polished, perfect, or advanced. It's just honest.

LESSON ONE

A HEART CONDITION

REFLECTION

Begin your study by sharing thoughts on this question.

1. Think of a friend who knows you well. How would that person describe you?

_____

_____

_____

BIBLE READING

Read Psalm 1:1–6 from the NCV or the NKJV.

NCV	NKJV
¹ Happy are those who don't listen to the wicked, who don't go where sinners go, who don't do what evil people do. ² They love the LORD's teachings, and they think about those teachings day and night. ³ They are strong, like a tree planted by a river. The tree produces fruit in season,	¹ Blessed is the man Who walks not in the counsel of the ungodly, Nor stands in the path of sinners, Nor sits in the seat of the scornful; ² But his delight is in the law of the LORD, And in His law he meditates day and night. ³ He shall be like a tree Planted by the rivers of water,

NCV

and its leaves don't die.
Everything they do will succeed.

⁴But wicked people are not like that.
They are like chaff that the wind blows
away.
⁵So the wicked will not escape God's
punishment.
Sinners will not worship with God's
people.
⁶This is because the LORD takes care of his
people,
but the wicked will be destroyed.

NKJV

That brings forth its fruit in its season,
Whose leaf also shall not wither;
And whatever he does shall prosper.

⁴The ungodly are not so,
But are like the chaff which the wind drives
away.
⁵Therefore the ungodly shall not stand in the
judgment,
Nor sinners in the congregation of the
righteous.

⁶For the LORD knows the way of the
righteous,
But the way of the ungodly shall perish.

DISCOVERY

Explore the Bible reading by discussing these questions.

2. What is the difference between a good person and a wicked person?

_____

_____

_____

3. How can righteous people remain pure?

_____

_____

_____

4. What kind of fruit do God's people produce?

_____

_____

_____

5. What future awaits unrighteous people?

_____

_____

_____

6. What are the end results of righteous living and selfish living?

_____

_____

_____

INSPIRATION

Here is an uplifting thought from the *Inspirational Study Bible*.

The heart is the center of the spiritual life. If the fruit of a tree is bad, you don't try to fix the fruit; you treat the roots. And if a person's actions are evil, it's not enough to change habits; you have to go deeper. You have to go to the heart of the problem, which is the problem of the heart.

That is why the state of the heart is so critical. What is the state of yours? . . . The state of your heart dictates whether you harbor a grudge or give grace, seek self-pity or seek Christ, drink human misery or taste God's mercy. No wonder, then, the wise man begs, "Above all else, guard your heart."

David's prayer should be ours: "Create in me a pure heart, O God."

And Jesus' statement rings true: "Blessed are the pure in heart, for they shall see God."

Note the order of this beatitude: first purify the heart, then you will see God. Clean the refinery, and the result will be a pure product.

(from *The Applause of Heaven* by Max Lucado)

RESPONSE

Use these questions to share more deeply with each other.

7. Why is it important for us to guard our hearts?

_____

_____

_____

8. How can we evaluate the condition of our hearts?

_____

_____

_____

9. How can we protect ourselves from evil influences?

_____

_____

_____

PRAYER

Father, we know that selfishness doesn't belong in Christian hearts. May your Holy Word enlighten our hearts. Open our eyes to our weaknesses and give us the courage to change what needs to be changed. Help us to bear lasting fruit for your kingdom.

JOURNALING

Take a few moments to record your personal insights from this lesson.

In what area of my life do I need to experience God's purifying work?

ADDITIONAL QUESTIONS

10. What selfish habits or actions do you want to work on eliminating from your life?

_____

_____

_____

11. What fruit would you like God to produce in your life?

_____

_____

_____

12. When is it difficult for you to guard your heart?

_____

_____

_____

For more Bible passages about righteousness, see Proverbs 11:18; Hosea 10:12; Matthew 5:6; Romans 1:17; 2 Corinthians 5:21; Philippians 1:9–11; 1 Timothy 6:11; James 3:17, 18.

ADDITIONAL THOUGHTS

LESSON TWO

TRUSTING GOD

REFLECTION

Begin your study by sharing thoughts on this question.

1. Think of someone you know who has relied on God for help during a difficult time. How does that example encourage you?

_____

_____

_____

BIBLE READING

Read Psalm 16:1–11 from the NCV or the NKJV.

NCV	NKJV

¹Protect me, God,
    because I trust in you.
²I said to the LORD, "You are my LORD.
    Every good thing I have comes from
        you."
³As for the godly people in the world,
    they are the wonderful ones I enjoy.
⁴But those who turn to idols
    will have much pain.
	¹Preserve me, O God, for in You I put my
	    trust.
	
	²O my soul, you have said to the LORD,
	    "You are my LORD,
	    My goodness is nothing apart from You."
	³As for the saints who are on the earth,
	    "They are the excellent ones, in whom is all
	        my delight."

NCV

I will not offer blood to those idols
    or even speak their names.

5 No, the Lord is all I need.
    He takes care of me.
6 My share in life has been pleasant;
    my part has been beautiful.

7 I praise the Lord because he advises me.
    Even at night, I feel his leading.
8 I keep the Lord before me always.
    Because he is close by my side,
    I will not be hurt.
9 So I rejoice and am glad.
    Even my body has hope,
10 because you will not leave me in the grave.
    You will not let your holy one rot.
11 You will teach me how to live a holy life.
    Being with you will fill me with joy;
    at your right hand I will find pleasure
    forever.

NKJV

4 Their sorrows shall be multiplied who
    hasten after another god;
Their drink offerings of blood I will not
    offer,
Nor take up their names on my lips.

5 O Lord, You are the portion of my
    inheritance and my cup;
You maintain my lot.
6 The lines have fallen to me in pleasant
    places;
Yes, I have a good inheritance.

7 I will bless the Lord who has given me
    counsel;
My heart also instructs me in the night
    seasons.
8 I have set the Lord always before me;
Because He is at my right hand I shall not
    be moved.

9 Therefore my heart is glad, and my glory
    rejoices;
My flesh also will rest in hope.
10 For You will not leave my soul in Sheol,
Nor will You allow Your Holy One to see
    corruption.
11 You will show me the path of life;
In Your presence is fullness of joy;
At Your right hand are pleasures
    forevermore.

DISCOVERY

Explore the Bible reading by discussing these questions.

2. How can you demonstrate your trust in God?

_____

_____

_____

3. List some of the ways God cares for those who trust him.

_____

_____

_____

4. What kind of future awaits those who trust in God?

_____

_____

_____

5. What are the advantages of living in communion with God?

_____

_____

_____

6. What aspects of God's character does this psalm highlight?

_____

_____

_____

INSPIRATION

Here is an uplifting thought from the *Inspirational Study Bible*.

Two-year-old Sara sits on my lap. We are watching a comedy on television about a guy who has a mouse in his room. He is asleep. He opens one eye and finds himself peering into the face of the rodent. The camera gets eye-level with the mouse, and suddenly the screen is filled with two eyes, whiskers, and a twitching nose.

I laugh, but Sara panics. She turns away from the screen and buries her face in my shoulder. Her arms encircle my neck and clamp like a vise. Her little body grows rigid. She thinks the mouse is going to get her.

"It's ok, Sara," I assure her.

She won't let go. "It's only a picture."

She peers up at me with one eye and then burrows her nose back into my shirt.

"Mouse get me," she whimpers.

"There is nothing to be afraid of," I say. "It's only a pretend mouse."

I speak with confidence because I am confident. There is really nothing to fear. I know. I've seen big mice on picture screens before. I know they go away.

Sara doesn't. Two-year-olds don't under-stand the concept of television. As far as she knows, the rodent on the screen is about to bound out of the box and gobble her up. As far as she knows, the mouse will be there every time she comes into this room. As far as she knows, television sets are nothing more than glass cages that house giant mice. There *is* reason to be afraid.

So she is afraid.

But with time, I convince her. . . . Sara has gone from white-faced fear to peaceful chuckles in a few moments. Why? Because her father spoke and she believed.

Would that we would do the same. Got any giant mice on your screen? Got any fears that won't go away? Got any whiskered monsters staring at you?

I wish the fears were just television images. They aren't. They lurk in hospital rooms and funeral homes. They stare at us from divorce papers and eviction notices. They glare through the eyes of cruel parents or an abusive mate.

And we, like Sara, get frightened. But we,

unlike Sara, don't know where to turn. Why did Sara turn to her dad for comfort? Simple. She knows me. . . .

And because she knows me, she trusts me. Instinctively, she is aware that I know more than she. So when I tell her not to worry, she doesn't worry.

Instinctively, we should know that God knows more than we do. Common sense would tell us that He isn't afraid of the mice that roar in our world. . . .

He's been there before. He knows how these shows end. He knows that the worst fear the foe can throw is only a mirage. And He wants us to listen to His voice and trust Him—as Sara trusted me. . . .

There are times when mice roar. There are times when we need a strong pair of arms. You need to know that the arms of God are there.

(from *Tell Me the Story* by Max Lucado)

RESPONSE

Use these questions to share more deeply with each other.

7. Think of a time when you felt overwhelmed by fear. How did you cope?

_____

_____

_____

8. What keeps us from turning to God with our fears?

_____

_____

_____

9. How can you remind yourself of God's presence the next time you feel overcome by fear?

_____

_____

_____

PRAYER

Father, we work hard to appear calm on the outside, but we have our hidden fears. You know them. We're afraid of being alone. We're afraid of being jobless. We're afraid of pain. Father, we offer these fears to you. Teach us to trust you. Give us more courage as we look to you, the One who knows no fear.

JOURNALING

Take a few moments to record your personal insights from this lesson.

What fear or problem do I need to turn over to God?

ADDITIONAL QUESTIONS

10. How does fear affect your relationship with God?

_____

_____

_____

11. How does this passage change your attitude toward your present fears?

_____

_____

_____

12. What can you do to encourage others to trust God?

_____

_____

_____

For more Bible passages about trusting God, see Proverbs 3:5; Isaiah 26:3, 4; 50:10; Jeremiah 17:7, 8; Habakkuk 3:17–19; Romans 15:13; Hebrews 6:18, 19.

LESSON THREE

GOD'S LAW

REFLECTION

Begin your study by sharing thoughts on this question.

1. Think of a particular time when you were challenged or comforted by the Bible. How did that affect your life?

_____

_____

_____

BIBLE READING

Read Psalm 19:7–14 from the NCV or the NKJV.

NCV

[7] The teachings of the LORD are perfect;
   they give new strength.
The rules of the LORD can be trusted;
   they make plain people wise.
[8] The orders of the LORD are right;
   they make people happy.
The commands of the LORD are pure;
   they light up the way.

NKJV

[7] The law of the LORD is perfect, converting
   the soul;
The testimony of the LORD is sure, making
   wise the simple;
[8] The statutes of the LORD are right, rejoicing
   the heart;
The commandment of the LORD is pure,
   enlightening the eyes;

NCV

9 Respect for the LORD is good;
  it will last forever.
The judgments of the LORD are true;
  they are completely right.
10 They are worth more than gold,
  even the purest gold.
They are sweeter than honey,
  even the finest honey.
11 By them your servant is warned.
  Keeping them brings great reward.

12 People cannot see their own mistakes.
  Forgive me for my secret sins.
13 Keep me from the sins of pride;
  don't let them rule me.
Then I can be pure
  and innocent of the greatest of sins.

14 I hope my words and thoughts please you.
  LORD, you are my Rock, the one who
  saves me.

NKJV

9 The fear of the LORD is clean, enduring
  forever;
The judgments of the LORD are true and
  righteous altogether.
10 More to be desired are they than gold,
  Yea, than much fine gold; Sweeter also than
  honey and the honeycomb.
11 Moreover by them Your servant is warned,
  And in keeping them there is great reward.

12 Who can understand his errors?
  Cleanse me from secret faults.
13 Keep back Your servant also from
  presumptuous sins;
Let them not have dominion over me.
Then I shall be blameless,
And I shall be innocent of great
  transgression.
14 Let the words of my mouth and the
  meditation of my heart
Be acceptable in Your sight,
O LORD, my strength and my Redeemer.

DISCOVERY

Explore the Bible reading by discussing these questions.

2. In what ways can the Bible change your life?

_____

_____

_____

3. What results from obeying God's commands?

_____

_____

_____

4. List the words that the Psalmist used to describe God's teaching?

_____

_____

_____

5. What attitude should we have toward God's Word?

_____

_____

_____

6. How can sin rule over people?

_____

_____

_____

INSPIRATION

Here is an uplifting thought from the *Inspirational Study Bible.*

The Ten Commandments tell us not to covet or lust. However, all moral law is more than a test; it's for our own good. Every law which God has given has been for our benefit. If a person breaks it, he is not only rebelling against God, he is hurting himself. God gave "the law" because he loves man. It is for man's benefit. God's commandments were given to protect and promote man's happiness, not to restrict it. God wants the best for man. To ask God to revise his commandments would be to ask him to stop loving man. . . .

In our universe, we live under God's law. In the physical realm, the planets move in split-second precision. There is no guesswork in the galaxies. We see in nature that everything is part of a plan which is harmonious, orderly, and obedient. Could a God who made the physical universe be any less exacting in the higher spiritual and moral order? God loves us with an infinite love, but he cannot and will not approve of disorder. Consequently, he has laid down spiritual laws which, if obeyed, bring harmony and fulfillment, but, if disobeyed, bring discord and disorder.

(from *How to Be Born Again* by Billy Graham)

RESPONSE

Use these questions to share more deeply with each other.

7. How does God's teaching demonstrate God's love for us?

_____

_____

_____

8. What blessings have you enjoyed as a result of obeying God's Word?

_____

_____

_____

9. How can we show our love for God's law?

_____

_____

_____

PRAYER

Father, we're amazed at your love for us. You have shown us the way to find true happiness and fulfillment. You have shown us how precious your Word is. Enrich our conscience so that we may be faithful to obey you.

JOURNALING

Take a few moments to record your personal insights from this lesson.

In what areas of my life have I failed to respect God's law? How do I need to change?

ADDITIONAL QUESTIONS

10. In what situations are you tempted to break God's law?

_____

_____

_____

11. How can you gain strength from God's Word to overcome temptation?

_____

_____

_____

12. How would your life be different if you had never heard God's Word?

_____

_____

_____

For more Bible passages about God's law, see Exodus 15:26; 20:1–17;
Leviticus 20:22; Galatians 2:16.

ADDITIONAL THOUGHTS

LESSON FOUR

FINDING COMFORT AND REST

REFLECTION

Begin your study by sharing thoughts on this question.

1. Think of a time when you felt lonely or discouraged. Where did you turn for help?

_____

_____

_____

BIBLE READING

Read Psalm 23:1–6 from the NCV or the NKJV.

NCV

¹The LORD is my shepherd;
  I have everything I need.
²He lets me rest in green pastures.
    He leads me to calm water.
³He gives me new strength.
  He leads me on paths that are right for the
      good of his name.
⁴Even if I walk through a very dark valley,
    I will not be afraid, because you are
      with me.

NKJV

¹The LORD is my shepherd;
  I shall not want.
²He makes me to lie down in green pastures;
  He leads me beside the still waters.
³He restores my soul;
  He leads me in the paths of righteousness
  For His name's sake.

⁴Yea, though I walk through the valley of the
    shadow of death,

NCV

Your rod and your walking stick comfort
me.

⁵ You prepare a meal for me
in front of my enemies.
You pour oil on my head;
you fill my cup to overflowing.
⁶ Surely your goodness and love will be with
me all my life,
and I will live in the house of the Lord
forever.

NKJV

I will fear no evil;
For You are with me;
Your rod and Your staff, they comfort me.

⁵ You prepare a table before me in the
presence of my enemies;
You anoint my head with oil;
My cup runs over.
⁶ Surely goodness and mercy shall follow me
All the days of my life;
And I will dwell in the house of the Lord
Forever.

DISCOVERY

Explore the Bible reading by discussing these questions.

2. How is God like a shepherd?

_____

_____

_____

3. How are we like sheep?

_____

_____

_____

4. How does God care for the needs of his people?

_____

_____

_____

5. What attitude should we have toward hardship and pain?

_____

_____

_____

6. What kind of future can God's people expect?

_____

_____

_____

INSPIRATION

Here is an uplifting thought from the *Inspirational Study Bible.*

It is . . . weariness that makes the words of the carpenter so compelling. Listen to them. "Come to me, all you who are weary and burdened and I will give you rest."

Come to me. . . . The invitation is to come to him. Why him?

He offers the invitation as a penniless rabbi in an oppressed nation. He has no political office, no connections with the authorities in Rome. He hasn't written a best-seller or earned a diploma.

Yet, he dares to look into the leathery faces of farmers and tired faces of housewives and offer rest. He looks into the disillusioned eyes of a preacher or two from Jerusalem. He gazes into the cynical stare of a banker and the hungry eyes of a bartender and makes this paradoxical promise: "Take my yoke upon you and learn from me, for I am gentle and humble in heart, and you will find rest for your souls."

The people came. They came out of the cul-de-sacs and office complexes of their day. They brought him the burdens of their existence and he gave them, not religion, not doctrine, not systems, but rest.

As a result, they called him Lord.

As a result, they called him Savior.

Not so much because of what he said, but because of what he did.

What he did on the cross during six hours, one Friday. . . .

Jesus was the only man to walk God's earth who claimed to have an answer for man's burdens. "Come to me," he invited them.

My prayer is that you, too, will find rest. And that you will sleep like a baby.

(from *Six Hours One Friday*
by Max Lucado)

RESPONSE

Use these questions to share more deeply with each other.

7. How is Jesus' offer of rest relevant today?

_____

_____

_____

8. In what ways have you already experienced God's rest?

_____

_____

_____

9. What keeps us from fully enjoying the rest God gives?

_____

_____

_____

PRAYER

Father, you are God and Creator, but we come to you as lost sheep in need of a shepherd. We need you to hold and comfort us, and to give us the rest that only you can give. Heal our wounds and give us new strength to follow you.

JOURNALING

Take a few moments to record your personal insights from this lesson.

What burdens do I need to leave at Jesus' feet?

ADDITIONAL QUESTIONS

10. How have you recently experienced God's comfort or rest?

_____

_____

_____

11. David thought of God as his shepherd. What picture or comparison describes your relationship with God?

_____

_____

_____

12. In what area of your life do you need God's guidance?

_____

_____

_____

For more Bible passages about finding comfort and rest, see Exodus 33:14; Psalm 62:1; Isaiah 49:13; Jeremiah 6:16; 31:13; Matthew 11:28–30; 2 Corinthians 1:3, 4.

ADDITIONAL THOUGHTS

LESSON FIVE

FORGIVENESS

REFLECTION

Begin your study by sharing thoughts on this question.

1. Think of a time when you received forgiveness from a friend. How did you feel?

_____

_____

_____

BIBLE READING

Read Psalm 32:1–11 from the NCV or the NKJV.

NCV	NKJV
¹ Happy is the person whose sins are forgiven, whose wrongs are pardoned. ² Happy is the person whom the LORD does not consider guilty and in whom there is nothing false.	¹ Blessed is he whose transgression is forgiven, Whose sin is covered. ² Blessed is the man to whom the LORD does not impute iniquity, And in whose spirit there is no deceit.
³ When I kept things to myself, I felt weak deep inside me.	³ When I kept silent, my bones grew old Through my groaning all the day long.

NCV

I moaned all day long.
⁴Day and night you punished me.
My strength was gone as in the summer
heat. *Selah*
⁵Then I confessed my sins to you
and didn't hide my guilt.
I said, "I will confess my sins to the Lord,"
and you forgave my guilt. *Selah*

⁶For this reason, all who obey you
should pray to you while they still can.
When troubles rise like a flood,
they will not reach them.
⁷You are my hiding place.
You protect me from my troubles
and fill me with songs of salvation.
Selah

⁸The Lord says, "I will make you wise and
show you where to go.
I will guide you and watch over you.
⁹So don't be like a horse or donkey,
that doesn't understand.
They must be led with bits and reins,
or they will not come near you."

¹⁰Wicked people have many troubles,
but the Lord's love surrounds those who
trust him.
¹¹Good people, rejoice and be happy in the
Lord.
Sing all you whose hearts are right.

NKJV

⁴For day and night Your hand was heavy
upon me;
My vitality was turned into the drought of
summer. Selah
⁵I acknowledged my sin to You,
And my iniquity I have not hidden.
I said, "I will confess my transgressions to
the Lord,"
And You forgave the iniquity of my sin.
Selah

⁶For this cause everyone who is godly shall
pray to You
In a time when You may be found;
Surely in a flood of great waters
They shall not come near him.
⁷You are my hiding place;
You shall preserve me from trouble;
You shall surround me with songs of
deliverance. Selah

⁸I will instruct you and teach you in the way
you should go;
I will guide you with My eye.
⁹Do not be like the horse or like the mule,
Which have no understanding,
Which must be harnessed with bit and
bridle,
Else they will not come near you.

¹⁰Many sorrows shall be to the wicked;
But he who trusts in the Lord, mercy shall
surround him.
¹¹Be glad in the Lord and rejoice, you
righteous;
And shout for joy, all you upright in heart!

DISCOVERY

Explore the Bible reading by discussing these questions.

2. Why do you think people try to hide their sins from God?

_____

_____

_____

3. What happens when people try to hide their sins from God?

_____

_____

_____

4. How can people find relief from guilt?

_____

_____

_____

5. How does God respond to those who repent?

_____

_____

_____

6. How does God want people to react to his correction?

_____

_____

_____

INSPIRATION

Here is an uplifting thought from the *Inspirational Study Bible*.

To say "I believe in Jesus" is not enough. You must be willing to acknowledge Him as the most important person in your life. You must be willing to say, "I will do what He wants me to do above all else and above any demands that others may place upon me." If you will make that decision, I have great news for you— I can promise you a very positive self-image. When Jesus is the most important person in your life, you will soon come to define yourself in the same way that Jesus defines you. You will begin to think of yourself as He thinks of you. And Here is more good news: Jesus thinks you're great! He thinks you're terrific. He really does.

You say, "Not me, Tony. You don't know me or the sin in my life. There are things that I can never tell you. If you knew them it would cause you to view me with contempt."

We could compare horror stories. You could tell me how rotten you are and I could tell you how rotten I am and we could try to see which of us is worse. Both of us would end up in despair. But that's not what Jesus wants us to do. He wants us to realize that once we accept Him as our Savior and Lord, we stand before Him as perfect people. That's right! When Jesus looks at me, He doesn't see anything wrong with me at all. In the words of Scripture, "I'm clothed in His righteousness." The Bible says that my sin is blotted out. It is buried in the deepest sea; it is remembered no more.

(from *It's Friday, But Sunday's Comin'*
by Tony Campolo)

RESPONSE

Use these questions to share more deeply with each other.

7. What keeps people from accepting God's forgiveness?

_____

_____

_____

8. When have you experienced God's forgiveness?

_____

_____

_____

9. In what ways should this affect your relationships with others?

_____

_____

_____

PRAYER

Father, you know us early in the morning; you know us late at night. You know us when we're weak; you know us when we're strong. Help us when we try to hide our sins from you. Father, forgive us and transform us into your likeness. Remind us that you will always love us.

JOURNALING

Take a few moments to record your personal insights from this lesson.

What sins do I need to confess to God?

ADDITIONAL QUESTIONS

10. How has your relationship with Jesus changed the way you view yourself?

_____

_____

_____

11. What have you learned about responding to God's forgiveness?

_____

_____

_____

12. In what ways can you express your appreciation to God for his forgiveness?

_____

_____

_____

For more Bible passages about forgiveness, see Psalm 130:4; Matthew 6:12–15; 26:28; Luke 1:77; Acts 5:31; Ephesians 1:7; Colossians 1:13, 14; 1 John 1:9.

ADDITIONAL THOUGHTS

LESSON SIX

RESTING IN GOD

REFLECTION

Begin your study by sharing thoughts on this question.

1. What were some of your childhood fears? How did you get over those fears?

_____

_____

_____

BIBLE READING

Read Psalm 46:1–11 from the NCV or the NKJV.

NCV

¹God is our protection and our strength.
   He always helps in times of trouble.
²So we will not be afraid even if the earth shakes,
   or the mountains fall into the sea,
³even if the oceans roar and foam,

NKJV

¹God is our refuge and strength,
   A very present help in trouble.
²Therefore we will not fear,
   Even though the earth be removed,
   And though the mountains be carried into the midst of the sea;

NCV

or the mountains shake at the raging sea.
  Selah

⁴ There is a river that brings joy to the city of
    God,
  the holy place where God Most High
    lives.
⁵ God is in that city, and so it will not be
    shaken.
  God will help her at dawn.
⁶ Nations tremble and kingdoms shake.
  God shouts and the earth crumbles.
⁷ The LORD All-Powerful is with us;
  the God of Jacob is our defender. *Selah*

⁸ Come and see what the LORD has done,
  the amazing things he has done on the
    earth.
⁹ He stops wars everywhere on the earth.
  He breaks all bows and spears
  and burns up the chariots with fire.
¹⁰ God says, "Be quiet and know that I am
    God.
  I will be supreme over all the nations;
  I will be supreme in the earth."

¹¹ The LORD All-Powerful is with us;
  the God of Jacob is our defender. *Selah*

NKJV

³ Though its waters roar and be troubled,
  Though the mountains shake with its
    swelling.   Selah

⁴ There is a river whose streams shall make
    glad the city of God,
  The holy place of the tabernacle of the Most
    High.
⁵ God is in the midst of her, she shall not be
    moved;
  God shall help her, just at the break of
    dawn.
⁶ The nations raged, the kingdoms were
    moved;
  He uttered His voice, the earth melted.

⁷ The LORD of hosts is with us;
  The God of Jacob is our refuge.   Selah
⁸ Come, behold the works of the LORD,
  Who has made desolations in the earth.
⁹ He makes wars cease to the end of the
    earth;
  He breaks the bow and cuts the spear in
    two;
  He burns the chariot in the fire.

¹⁰ Be still, and know that I am God;
  I will be exalted among the nations,
  I will be exalted in the earth!

¹¹ The LORD of hosts is with us;
  The God of Jacob is our refuge.   Selah

DISCOVERY

Explore the Bible reading by discussing these questions.

2. How can you overcome fears?

_____

_____

_____

3. How does God protect his people?

_____

_____

_____

4. Why is this psalm comforting to you?

_____

_____

_____

5. How can remembering God's power bring us peace?

_____

_____

_____

6. What amazing things has God done for you?

_____

_____

_____

INSPIRATION

Here is an uplifting thought from the *Inspirational Study Bible.*

When I was ten years old, my mother enrolled me in piano lessons. Now, many youngsters excel at the keyboard. Not me. Spending thirty minutes every afternoon tethered to a piano bench was a torture just one level away from swallowing broken glass. The metronome inspected each second with glacial slowness before it was allowed to pass.

Some of the music, though, I learned to enjoy. I hammered the staccatos. I belabored the crescendos. . . . But there was one instruction in the music I could never obey to my teacher's satisfaction. The rest. The zigzagged command to do nothing. Nothing! What sense does that make? Why sit at the piano and pause when you can pound?

"Because," my teacher patiently explained, "music is always sweeter after a rest."

It didn't make sense to me at age ten. But now, a few decades later, the words ring with wisdom—divine wisdom.

(from *The Applause of Heaven* by Max Lucado)

RESPONSE

Use these questions to share more deeply with each other.

7. What does it mean to be still before God?

_____

_____

_____

8. What happens when we don't take time to be quiet before God?

_____

_____

_____

9. What keeps you from spending time with God?

_____

_____

_____

PRAYER

Father, you have done amazing things. Open our eyes to your power and wonders. Keep our focus on your greatness rather than on our weakness. Father, teach us to be quiet before you. Only as we sit at your feet will our fears be transformed into faith.

JOURNALING

Take a few moments to record your personal insights from this lesson.

When can I set aside some time to be quiet before God?

ADDITIONAL QUESTIONS

10. What fears do you have?

_____

_____

_____

11. What advice would you offer a friend who is overwhelmed by fear or anxiety?

_____

_____

_____

12. How would you describe God's power and protection?

_____

_____

_____

For more Bible passages about resting in God, see Deuteronomy 33:12; Psalm 23:2; 62:5; 91:1; Isaiah 30:15; Zephaniah 3:17.

ADDITIONAL THOUGHTS

LESSON SEVEN

DEALING WITH GUILT

REFLECTION

Begin your study by sharing thoughts on this question.

1. Think of a time when you received something you did not deserve. How did you respond?

_____

_____

_____

BIBLE READING

Read Psalm 51:1–12 from the NCV or the NKJV.

NCV

¹God, be merciful to me
   because you are loving.
   Because you are always ready to be
      merciful,
      wipe out all my wrongs.
²Wash away all my guilt
   and make me clean again.

³I know about my wrongs,
   and I can't forget my sin.

NKJV

¹Have mercy upon me, O God,
   According to Your lovingkindness;
   According to the multitude of Your tender
      mercies,
   Blot out my transgressions.
²Wash me thoroughly from my iniquity,
   And cleanse me from my sin.

³For I acknowledge my transgressions,
   And my sin is always before me.

NCV

⁴You are the only one I have sinned against;
    I have done what you say is wrong.
You are right when you speak
    and fair when you judge.
⁵I was brought into this world in sin.
    In sin my mother gave birth to me.

⁶You want me to be completely truthful,
    so teach me wisdom.
⁷Take away my sin, and I will be clean.
    Wash me, and I will be whiter than
      snow.
⁸Make me hear sounds of joy and gladness;
    let the bones you crushed be happy
      again.
⁹Turn your face from my sins
    and wipe out all my guilt.

¹⁰Create in me a pure heart, God,
    and make my spirit right again.
¹¹Do not send me away from you
    or take your Holy Spirit away from me.
¹²Give me back the joy of your salvation.
    Keep me strong by giving me a willing
      spirit.

NKJV

⁴Against You, You only, have I sinned,
    And done this evil in Your sight—
That You may be found just when You
      speak,
    And blameless when You judge.

⁵Behold, I was brought forth in iniquity,
    And in sin my mother conceived me.
⁶Behold, You desire truth in the inward
      parts,
    And in the hidden part You will make me to
      know wisdom.

⁷Purge me with hyssop, and I shall be clean;
    Wash me, and I shall be whiter than snow.
⁸Make me hear joy and gladness,
    That the bones You have broken may
      rejoice.
⁹Hide Your face from my sins,
    And blot out all my iniquities.

¹⁰Create in me a clean heart, O God,
    And renew a steadfast spirit within me.
¹¹Do not cast me away from Your presence,
    And do not take Your Holy Spirit from me.

¹²Restore to me the joy of Your salvation,
    And uphold me by Your generous Spirit.

DISCOVERY

Explore the Bible reading by discussing these questions.

2. List the attributes of God described in this Psalm.

_____

_____

_____

3. What does God think of our sins?

_____

_____

_____

4. How did David, the psalm writer, react to God's correction?

_____

_____

_____

5. What did David ask God to do for him?

_____

_____

_____

6. What does God do for a person who repents of sin?

_____

_____

_____

INSPIRATION

Here is an uplifting thought from the *Inspirational Study Bible.*

Man by himself cannot deal with his own guilt. He must have help from the outside. In order to forgive himself, he must have forgiveness from the one he has offended. Yet man is unworthy to ask God for forgiveness. . . .

You can't do that by yourself. I don't care how many worship services you attend or good deeds you do, your goodness is insufficient. You *can't* be good enough to deserve forgiveness. No one bats a thousand. No one bowls three hundred. No one. Not you, not me, not anyone. . . .

Listen. Quit trying to quench your own guilt. You can't do it. There is no way. Not with a bottle of whiskey or perfect Sunday School attendance. Sorry. I don't care how bad you are. You can't be bad enough to forget it. And I don't care how good you are. You can't be good enough to overcome it.

You need a Savior.

(from *No Wonder They Call Him the Savior* by Max Lucado)

RESPONSE

Use these questions to share more deeply with each other.

7. How does God convict us of sin?

_____

_____

_____

8. How do people try to cope with guilt?

_____

_____

_____

9. What does this psalm say about dealing with guilt?

_____

_____

_____

PRAYER

Father, we thank you for your great love for sinners. No one has committed too great a sin for you to forgive. We submit to your convicting work—expose the sin in our hearts and lead us to repentance. We long to experience the joy of your salvation.

JOURNALING

Write a prayer that praises God for removing your guilt.

ADDITIONAL QUESTIONS

10. How do we tend to react to discipline? Why?

_____

_____

_____

11. What sins are difficult for you to resist?

_____

_____

_____

12. How can you become free of guilt?

_____

_____

_____

For more Bible passages about dealing with guilt, see Ezra 9:5–7; Nehemiah 1:5–7; Psalm 32:5; 38:4–18; Acts 19:18; Hebrews 10:19–22; James 5:16; 1 John 1:9.

ADDITIONAL THOUGHTS

LESSON EIGHT

TRUE HAPPINESS

REFLECTION

Begin your study by sharing thoughts on this question.

1. What is your favorite hobby or activity? Why do you enjoy it?

_____

_____

_____

BIBLE READING

Read Psalm 62:1–12 from the NCV or the NKJV.

NCV

[1] I find rest in God; only he can save me.
[2] He is my rock and my salvation.
   He is my defender;
   I will not be defeated.

[3] How long will you attack someone?
   Will all of you kill that person?
   Who is like a leaning wall, like a fence
      ready to fall?

NKJV

[1] Truly my soul silently waits for God;
   From Him comes my salvation.
[2] He only is my rock and my salvation;
   He is my defense;
   I shall not be greatly moved.

[3] How long will you attack a man?
   You shall be slain, all of you,
   Like a leaning wall and a tottering fence.

NCV

4 They are planning to make that person fall.
   They enjoy telling lies.
With their mouths they bless,
   but in their hearts they curse.   *Selah*

5 I find rest in God;
   only he gives me hope.
6 He is my rock and my salvation.
   He is my defender;
      I will not be defeated.
7 My honor and salvation come from God.
   He is my mighty rock and my
      protection.

8 People, trust God all the time.
   Tell him all your problems,
   because God is our protection.   *Selah*

9 The least of people are only a breath,
   and even the greatest are just a lie.
On the scales, they weigh nothing;
   together they are only a breath.
10 Do not trust in force.
   Stealing is of no use.
Even if you gain more riches,
   don't put your trust in them.

11 God has said this,
   and I have heard it over and over:
   God is strong.
12 The LORD is loving.
   You reward people for what they have
      done.

NKJV

4 They only consult to cast him down from
      his high position;
They delight in lies;
They bless with their mouth,
But they curse inwardly.   Selah

5 My soul, wait silently for God alone,
   For my expectation is from Him.
6 He only is my rock and my salvation;
   He is my defense;
   I shall not be moved.
7 In God is my salvation and my glory;
   The rock of my strength,
   And my refuge, is in God.

8 Trust in Him at all times, you people;
   Pour out your heart before Him;
   God is a refuge for us.   Selah

9 Surely men of low degree are a vapor,
   Men of high degree are a lie;
   If they are weighed on the scales,
   They are altogether lighter than vapor.
10 Do not trust in oppression,
   Nor vainly hope in robbery;
   If riches increase,
   Do not set your heart on them.

11 God has spoken once,
   Twice I have heard this:
   That power belongs to God.
12 Also to You, O LORD, belongs mercy;
   For You render to each one according to his
      work.

DISCOVERY

Explore the Bible reading by discussing these questions.

2. List the images from this psalm that show the psalmist's confidence in God.

_____

_____

_____

3. How does God protect his people?

_____

_____

_____

4. How does this psalm encourage you to deal with problems and pain?

_____

_____

_____

5. What does this passage reveal about the value of power, wealth, and status?

_____

_____

_____

6. How does God reward his people?

_____

_____

_____

INSPIRATION

Here is an uplifting thought from the *Inspirational Study Bible.*

The only ultimate disaster that can befall us, I have come to realize, is to feel ourselves to be home on earth. As long as we are aliens, we cannot forget our true homeland.

Unhappiness on earth cultivates a hunger for heaven. By gracing us with a deep dissatisfaction, God holds our attention. The only tragedy, then, is to be satisfied prematurely. To settle for earth. To be content in a strange land. . . .

We are not happy here because we are not at home here. We are not happy here because we are not supposed to be happy here. We are "like foreigners and strangers in this world" (1 Pet. 2:11).

Take a fish and place him on the beach. Watch his gills gasp and scales dry. Is he happy? No! How do you make him happy? Do you cover him with a mountain of cash? Do

you get a beach chair and sunglasses? Do you bring him a *Playfish* magazine and martini? Do you wardrobe him in double breasted fins and people-skinned shoes?

Of course not. Then how do you make him happy? You put him back in his element. You put him back in the water. He will never be happy on the beach simply because he was not made for the beach.

And you will never be completely happy on earth simply because you were not made for earth. Oh, you will have moments of joy. You will catch glimpses of light. You will know moments or even days of peace. But they simply do not compare with the happiness that lies ahead.

(from *When God Whispers Your Name* by Max Lucado)

RESPONSE

Use these questions to share more deeply with each other.

7. Where do people look for satisfaction?

_____

_____

_____

8. What happens to us when we depend on people or objects to make us happy?

_____

_____

_____

9. When are you most likely to feel "at home" on earth?

_____

_____

_____

PRAYER

We know, Father, that someday you are going to take all of your followers into eternal happiness. It is to that day that we look, and it is upon our hope and confidence that you will return, that we stand.

JOURNALING

How can I demonstrate unfailing trust in God alone?

ADDITIONAL QUESTIONS

10. How is the happiness that God gives different from what the world offers?

_____

_____

_____

11. What steps can you take to overcome selfish desires?

_____

_____

_____

12. How does your confidence in God help you face life's challenges?

_____

_____

_____

For more Bible passages about finding true happiness, see Psalm 126:2–6; 145:19; Habakkuk 3:17–19; Philippians 4:11, 12; 1 Timothy 6:6–8.

ADDITIONAL THOUGHTS

LESSON NINE

A FRESH PERSPECTIVE

REFLECTION

Begin your study by sharing thoughts on this question.

1. How do you cheer yourself up when you feel discontent or dissatisfied?

_____

_____

_____

BIBLE READING

Read Psalm 90:1–12 from the NCV or the NKJV.

NCV

¹ LORD, you have been our home
  since the beginning.
² Before the mountains were born
    and before you created the earth and the
      world,
you are God.
    You have always been, and you will
      always be.

NKJV

¹ LORD, You have been our dwelling place in
      all generations.
² Before the mountains were brought
      forth,
Or ever You had formed the earth and the
      world,
Even from everlasting to everlasting, You
      are God.

NCV

³ You turn people back into dust.
  You say, "Go back into dust, human
    beings."
⁴ To you, a thousand years
  is like the passing of a day,
  or like a few hours in the night.
⁵ While people sleep, you take their lives.
  They are like grass that grows up in the
    morning.
⁶ In the morning they are fresh and new,
  but by evening they dry up and die.

⁷ We are destroyed by your anger;
  we are terrified by your hot anger.
⁸ You have put the evil we have done right in
    front of you;
  you clearly see our secret sins.
⁹ All our days pass while you are angry.
  Our years end with a moan.
¹⁰ Our lifetime is seventy years
  or, if we are strong, eighty years.
  But the years are full of hard work and
    pain.
  They pass quickly, and then we are gone.

¹¹ Who knows the full power of your anger?
  Your anger is as great as our fear of you
    should be.
¹² Teach us how short our lives really are
  so that we may be wise.

NKJV

³ You turn man to destruction,
  And say, "Return, O children of men."
⁴ For a thousand years in Your sight
  Are like yesterday when it is past,
  And like a watch in the night.
⁵ You carry them away like a flood;
  They are like a sleep.
  In the morning they are like grass which
    grows up:
⁶ In the morning it flourishes and grows up;
  In the evening it is cut down and withers.

⁷ For we have been consumed by Your anger,
  And by Your wrath we are terrified.
⁸ You have set our iniquities before You,
  Our secret sins in the light of Your
    countenance.
⁹ For all our days have passed away in Your
    wrath;
  We finish our years like a sigh.
¹⁰ The days of our lives are seventy years;
  And if by reason of strength they are eighty
    years,
  Yet their boast is only labor and sorrow;
  For it is soon cut off, and we fly away.
¹¹ Who knows the power of Your anger?
  For as the fear of You, so is Your wrath.
¹² So teach us to number our days,
  That we may gain a heart of wisdom.

DISCOVERY

Explore the Bible reading by discussing these questions.

2. What did the psalmist want his readers to understand about God? About themselves? About life?

_____

_____

_____

3. How does this passage contrast God with people?

_____

_____

_____

4. Why does God address the sin of people?

_____

_____

_____

5. What does it mean to fear God?

_____

_____

_____

6. Why is it important to remember that life is short?

_____

_____

_____

INSPIRATION

Here is an uplifting thought from the *Inspirational Study Bible.*

Psalm 90 is the only psalm specifically attributed to Moses. He may have written others, but we know for sure he wrote this one. Remember Moses? Most think of him as a man of action, an aggressive leader, point man in the exodus, outspoken giver of the law. But it is easy to overlook the repetitious, monotonous routine he endured. Between ages forty and eighty, Moses led his father-in-law's flock of sheep in the desert. Following the exodus, he led the Hebrews for another forty years as they wandered across and around the wilderness. I'd say he knew about the blahs. Same terrain, same scenes, same route, same ornery people, same negative outlook, same complaints, same miserable weather, same everything! The prayer he wrote could have been his means of maintaining sanity! . . .

Frequently, our problem with boredom begins when we fall under monotony's "spell." . . .

How to cope? We must direct our attention (as Moses does) to (a) the right object and (b) the right perspective. . . .

As I probe my soul during times of such wrestling, almost without exception, I find three thoughts washing around in my head. First, I think: Life is so short. . . . Look again at Moses' prayer. He brings a second thought that plagues me when the blahs come: My sins are so obvious. . . .

Yes, life is short. Yes, our sins are obvious. . . . And if those thoughts aren't hard enough to handle, there is a third feeling: My days are so empty. . . . After the satisfaction that comes from fresh joy in the morning, there is restoration. . . . God has a way of balancing out the good with the bad.

(from *Living Above the Level of Mediocrity* by Charles Swindoll)

RESPONSE

Use these questions to share more deeply with each other.

7. Why do some people feel discontent and disillusioned?

_____

_____

_____

8. How does this passage encourage us to cope with the monotony of life?

_____

_____

_____

9. What steps can you take that will refresh you when you grow discouraged?

_____

_____

_____

PRAYER

Father, the monotony of life can lull us into a sense of dissatisfaction and futility. In those times, remind us that you are in control and you have a purpose for us. Give us your perspective of what is important and help us to invest our time wisely. Take our feeble efforts and transform them into works that last for eternity.

JOURNALING

Take a few moments to record your personal insights from this lesson.

What new insight about God or myself have I gained from this passage?

ADDITIONAL QUESTIONS

10. How do we try to hide our sins from God? Why?

_____

_____

_____

11. Why should we be honest with ourselves and God about our failures?

_____

_____

_____

12. What causes you to worry about your future?

_____

_____

_____

For more Bible passages about finding a fresh perspective, see Matthew 6:19–21; John 4:35–38; 15:16; Colossians 1:10–12; 1 Timothy 4:16; 6:17–19; 2 Thessalonians 1:11; Hebrews 10:34–36.

ADDITIONAL THOUGHTS

LESSON TEN

REMEMBERING THE IMPORTANT THINGS

REFLECTION

Begin your study by sharing thoughts on this question.

1. If you were asked to list your priorities, what would they be?

_____

_____

_____

BIBLE READING

Read Psalm 103:1-14 from the NCV or the NKJV.

NCV

[1] My whole being, praise the LORD;
  all my being, praise his holy name.
[2] My whole being, praise the LORD
    and do not forget all his kindnesses.
[3] He forgives all my sins
    and heals all my diseases.
[4] He saves my life from the grave
    and loads me with love and mercy.
[5] He satisfies me with good things
    and makes me young again, like the eagle.

NKJV

[1] Bless the LORD, O my soul;
  And all that is within me, bless His holy
    name!
[2] Bless the LORD, O my soul,
  And forget not all His benefits:
[3] Who forgives all your iniquities,
  Who heals all your diseases,
[4] Who redeems your life from destruction,
  Who crowns you with lovingkindness and
    tender mercies,

NCV

⁶The LORD does what is right and fair
     for all who are wronged by others.
⁷He showed his ways to Moses
     and his deeds to the people of Israel.
⁸The LORD shows mercy and is kind.
     He does not become angry quickly, and
          he has great love.
⁹He will not always accuse us,
     and he will not be angry forever.
¹⁰He has not punished us as our sins should
          be punished;
     he has not repaid us for the evil we have
          done.
¹¹As high as the sky is above the earth,
     so great is his love for those who respect
          him.
¹²He has taken our sins away from us
     as far as the east is from west.
¹³The LORD has mercy on those who respect
          him,
     as a father has mercy on his children.
¹⁴He knows how we were made;
     he remembers that we are dust.

NKJV

⁵Who satisfies your mouth with good
          things,
     So that your youth is renewed like the
          eagle's.

⁶The LORD executes righteousness
     And justice for all who are oppressed.
⁷He made known His ways to Moses,
     His acts to the children of Israel.
⁸The LORD is merciful and gracious,
     Slow to anger, and abounding in mercy.
⁹He will not always strive with us,
     Nor will He keep His anger forever.
¹⁰He has not dealt with us according to our
          sins,
     Nor punished us according to our
          iniquities.

¹¹For as the heavens are high above the earth,
     So great is His mercy toward those who fear
          Him;
¹²As far as the east is from the west,
     So far has He removed our transgressions
          from us.
¹³As a father pities his children,
     So the LORD pities those who fear Him.
¹⁴For He knows our frame;
     He remembers that we are dust.

DISCOVERY

Explore the Bible reading by discussing these questions.

2. What is praise? Name some ways we can praise God.

_____

_____

_____

3. What human needs does God meet?

_____

_____

_____

4. How does God reveal himself to us?

_____

_____

_____

5. Why doesn't God give us what we deserve?

_____

_____

_____

6. Who receives God's mercy and compassion? Why?

_____

_____

_____

INSPIRATION

Here is an uplifting thought from the *Inspirational Study Bible.*

Abraham Lincoln once listened to the pleas of the mother of a soldier who'd been sentenced to hang for treason. She begged the President to grant a pardon. Lincoln agreed. Yet, he's reported to have left the lady with the following words: "Still, I wish we could teach him a lesson. I wish we could give him just a little bit of a hangin'. "

I think I know what the old rail-splitter had in mind. Yesterday, I got a little bit of hangin'.

We were having Sunday lunch at the home of a fellow missionary family. It was after the meal . . . . Their three-year-old daughter Beth Ann was playing with our two-year-old Jenna in the front yard. All of a sudden Beth Ann rushed in with a look of panic on her face. "Jenna is in the pool!"

Paul was the first to arrive at the poolside . . . and lifted her up out of the water to the extended hands of her mother. Jenna was simultaneously choking, crying, and coughing. She vomited a bellyful of water. I held her as she cried. Denalyn began to weep. I began to sweat.

For the rest of the day I couldn't hold her enough, nor could we thank Beth Ann enough . . . . I still can't thank God enough.

It was a little bit of hangin'.

The stool was kicked out from under my feet and the rope jerked around my neck just long enough to remind me of what really matters. It was a divine slap, a gracious knock on the head, a severe mercy. Because of it, I came face to face with one of the underground's slyest agents—the agent of familiarity. . . .

To say that this agent of familiarity breeds contempt is to let him off easy. Contempt is just one of his offspring. He also sires broken hearts, wasted hours, and an insatiable desire for more. . . . He won't take your children, he'll just make you too busy to notice them. His whispers to procrastinate are seductive. There is always next summer to coach the team, next month to go to the lake, and next week to teach Johnny how to pray. He'll make you forget that the faces around your table will soon be at tables of their own. Hence, books will go unread, games will go unplayed, hearts will go unnurtured, and opportunities will go ignored. All because the poison of the ordinary has deadened your senses to the magic of the moment. . . .

On a shelf above my desk is a picture of two

little girls. They're holding hands and standing in front of a swimming pool, the same pool from which the younger of the two had been pulled only minutes before. I put the picture where I would see it daily so I would remember what God doesn't want me to forget.

And you can bet this time I'm going to remember. I don't want any more hangin'. Not even a little bit.

(from *God Came Near*
by Max Lucado)

RESPONSE

Use these questions to share more deeply with each other.

7. How does familiarity divert our focus from life's most important things?

_____

_____

_____

8. What happens when we neglect the important things in life?

_____

_____

9. What does this psalm remind you to do?

_____

_____

_____

PRAYER

Father, had you not become flesh and dwelt among us, had you not treated us with mercy and kindness, had you not loved us beyond our worth, you would still be God. You would still be holy. And you would still be worthy of our praise. We thank you and worship your holy name forever and ever.

JOURNALING

Take a few moments to record your personal insights from this lesson.

What are the most important things in my life? What changes could I make to reflect those priorities?

ADDITIONAL QUESTIONS

10. Why do we sometimes fail to praise God?

_____

_____

_____

11. What do we gain when we praise God?

_____

_____

_____

12. How can you remember to praise God this week for what he has done for you?

_____

_____

_____

For more Bible passages about praising God, see Deuteronomy 6:10–13;
1 Chronicles 16:9–12; Job 36:24; Psalm 33:1; 77:11; 147:1.

LESSON ELEVEN

GOD SAVES AND PROTECTS

REFLECTION

Begin your study by sharing thoughts on this question.

1. When did Jesus become your Savior? What led to your decision?

_____

_____

_____

BIBLE READING

Read Psalm 125:1–126:6 from the NCV or the NKJV.

NCV	NKJV

[1] Those who trust the LORD are like Mount Zion,
    which sits unmoved forever.
[2] As the mountains surround Jerusalem,
    the LORD surrounds his people
    now and forever.
 	
[3] The wicked will not rule
    over those who do right.
	[1] Those who trust in the LORD
	    Are like Mount Zion,
	    Which cannot be moved, but abides
	        forever.
	[2] As the mountains surround Jerusalem,
	    So the LORD surrounds His people
	    From this time forth and forever.
	
	[3] For the scepter of wickedness shall not rest

NCV

If they did, the people who do right
    might use their power to do evil.

4 LORD, be good to those who are good,
    whose hearts are honest.
5 But, LORD, when you remove those who do
    evil,
    also remove those who stop following
    you.

Let there be peace in Israel.

Psalm 126
1 When the LORD brought the prisoners back
    to Jerusalem,
  it seemed as if we were dreaming.
2 Then we were filled with laughter,
    and we sang happy songs.
Then the other nations said,
    "The LORD has done great things for
    them."
3 The LORD has done great things for us,
    and we are very glad.

4 LORD, return our prisoners again,
    as you bring streams to the desert.
5 Those who cry as they plant crops
    will sing at harvest time.
6 Those who cry
    as they carry out the seeds
will return singing
    and carrying bundles of grain.

NKJV

On the land allotted to the righteous,
Lest the righteous reach out their hands to
    iniquity.

4 Do good, O LORD, to those who are good,
And to those who are upright in their
    hearts.

5 As for such as turn aside to their crooked
    ways,
The LORD shall lead them away
With the workers of iniquity.

Peace be upon Israel!

Psalm 126
1 When the LORD brought back the captivity
    of Zion,
We were like those who dream.
2 Then our mouth was filled with laughter,
And our tongue with singing.
Then they said among the nations,
  "The LORD has done great things for them."
3 The LORD has done great things for us,
And we are glad.

4 Bring back our captivity, O LORD,
As the streams in the South.

5 Those who sow in tears
Shall reap in joy.
6 He who continually goes forth weeping,
Bearing seed for sowing,
Shall doubtless come again with rejoicing,
Bringing his sheaves with him.

DISCOVERY

Explore the Bible reading by discussing these questions.

2. How can people receive God's protection?

_____

_____

_____

3. What does the psalmist ask God to do to the righteous? To the wicked?

_____

_____

_____

4. Why can we be confident that good will ultimately defeat evil?

_____

_____

_____

5. How does God want us to respond to his salvation and protection?

_____

_____

_____

6. What happens when people publicly acknowledge what God has done for them?

_____

_____

_____

INSPIRATION

Here is an uplifting thought from the *Inspirational Study Bible.*

God has done everything possible to bring you salvation; you can add nothing to what He has done. He has shown us the vision of the coming storm to give advance warning of the judgment so that we can flee from His wrath and come to Him. If you wish to be saved and go to heaven, you can, by believing in the Lord Jesus Christ as your Savior.

Jesus Christ rose from the dead to be alive forever. Because He is alive and because He can be everywhere at once, He is right there where you're reading. All you have to do is take Him, receive Him, accept Him personally into your heart as your Lord and Savior. . . .

What more could you desire, ask, or ever hope for than that the grace of our Lord Jesus Christ be with you forever?

(from *Storm Warning*
by Billy Graham)

RESPONSE

Use these questions to share more deeply with each other.

7. What protection does God offer from the coming judgment?

_____

_____

_____

8. What causes some people to hesitate to accept God's offer of salvation?

_____

_____

_____

9. What prompted you to seek God's forgiveness and salvation?

_____

_____

_____

PRAYER

Father, our hearts are filled with joy because of the great things you have done for us. We thank you for your salvation and constant protection. We offer you our praise, adoration, and thanksgiving.

JOURNALING

Take a few moments to record your personal insights from this lesson.

Write a prayer of praise for God's salvation.

ADDITIONAL QUESTIONS

10. How do people try to earn their way to heaven?

_____

_____

_____

11. Why is it difficult to accept salvation as a *free* gift?

_____

_____

_____

12. Which of your friends or co-workers does not fully understand God's plan of salvation? How can you share the gospel with that person?

_____

_____

_____

For more Bible passages about salvation, see 1 Chronicles 16:23; Psalm 40:10, 16; 69:29; Isaiah 12:2; Jonah 2:9; Acts 4:12; 1 Thessalonians 5:9; Revelation 7:10.

ADDITIONAL THOUGHTS

LESSON TWELVE

THE HAPPY HOME

REFLECTION

Begin your study by sharing thoughts on this question.

1. Think of one of your favorite childhood memories. Why is that memory special to you?

_____

_____

_____

BIBLE READING

Read Psalm 128:1-6 from the NCV or the NKJV.

NCV

¹ Happy are those who respect the LORD and obey him.
² You will enjoy what you work for,
   and you will be blessed with good things.
³ Your wife will give you many children,
   like a vine that produces much fruit.
Your children will bring you much good,
   like olive branches that produce many olives.

NKJV

¹ Blessed is every one who fears the LORD,
   Who walks in His ways.

² When you eat the labor of your hands,
   You shall be happy, and it shall be well with you.
³ Your wife shall be like a fruitful vine
   In the very heart of your house,
   Your children like olive plants
   All around your table.

NCV	NKJV
⁴This is how the man who respects the LORD will be blessed. ⁵May the LORD bless you from Mount Zion; may you enjoy the good things of Jerusalem all your life. ⁶May you see your grandchildren. Let there be peace in Israel.	⁴Behold, thus shall the man be blessed Who fears the LORD. ⁵The LORD bless you out of Zion, And may you see the good of Jerusalem All the days of your life. ⁶Yes, may you see your children's children. Peace be upon Israel!

DISCOVERY

Explore the Bible reading by discussing these questions.

2. How can families receive God's blessing?

_____

_____

_____

3. List the blessings that God gives to his children.

_____

_____

_____

4. What does God think of children?

_____

_____

_____

5. What good things does God want families to enjoy?

_____

_____

_____

6. How can families determine whether God is the head of their home?

_____

_____

_____

INSPIRATION

Here is an uplifting thought from the *Inspirational Study Bible*.

Perhaps the most taxing of all, are the years a family finds itself in and out of crisis situations. Little babies that cooed and gurgled grow up into challenging, independent-thinking adolescents. The protective, sheltered environment of the home is broken into by the school, new friends, alien philosophies, financial strain, illness, accidents, hard questions, constant decisions, and busy schedules. . . and it isn't difficult to feel the pressure mounting—especially when you add dating, new drivers in the family, leaving for college, talk of marriage, and moving out. Whew! And what does God say about these years? . . .

He says we'll be "blessed." We'll be "happy." It will "be well" with us during these years. . . . In the family portrayed on this scriptural canvas, "the Lord" is still central. . . .

Even before you finish, . . . it may be the right time for you to come to terms with the truth regarding your family. I must be honest with you, in most of the family conflicts I have dealt with involving trouble with teenagers, the problem has been more with parents who were either too liberal and permissive or too inflexible, distant, rigid (and sometimes hypocritical) than with teenagers who were unwilling to cooperate. When the modeling is as it should be, there is seldom much trouble from those who fall under the shadow of the leader. Strengthening your grip on the family may start with an unguarded appraisal of the leadership your family is expected to follow.

(from *Strengthening Your Grip* by Charles Swindoll)

RESPONSE

Use these questions to share more deeply with each other.

7.   What are some of the problems families face today?

_____

_____

_____

8. How can families work to strengthen family relationships?

_____

_____

_____

9. What encouragement can families glean from this psalm?

_____

_____

_____

PRAYER

God, give us strength as we try to be more like Jesus in our homes. We ask you to keep the evil one away from us; draw us into close communion with you. Let our families be testimonies of your love for us, so that when people look at us, they will see how you have loved the world.

JOURNALING

Take a few moments to record your personal insights from this lesson.

How can I ensure that God is the head of my home?

ADDITIONAL QUESTIONS

10. What happens to families who don't follow God's ways?

_____
_____
_____

11. How can parents teach their children to respect God?

_____
_____
_____

12. How has God blessed your family? How can you praise him for his blessings?

_____
_____
_____

For more Bible passages about the family, see Genesis 2:18–24; Exodus 20:12; Matthew 19:5, 6; Ephesians 5:22–6:4.

ADDITIONAL THOUGHTS

LEADERS' NOTES

LESSON ONE

This psalm contrasts the life of a righteous person with the life of an unrighteous person. Encourage participants to keep this theme in mind as you go through the lesson.

Question 4: Ask a group member to read aloud these related verses: John 15:5, 16; Galatians 5:22.

Question 6: The answer to this question is given in the text, but we can also see the results of righteous and selfish living by looking at the lives of people around us.

Question 8: Remind group members that they can help one another recognize and eliminate sinful habits from their lives. The first step toward helping each other may be to brainstorm practical answers to question 9.

LESSON TWO

In this psalm, David highlights the advantages of living in communion with God. This psalm is also quoted in the New Testament as a reference to the resurrection of Jesus Christ (Acts 2:25–28, 31; 13:35–37).

Question 3: God does not promise to save his people from life's trials and struggles, but he does care for us in the midst of our problems. Ask participants to share one way they have experienced God's care.

Question 7: Group members may feel uncomfortable telling others about their fears. You may want to share a personal story to create an atmosphere of openness and honesty.

LESSON THREE

This psalm focuses on three ways God reveals himself to people: God shows his greatness through nature (vs. 1–6); God reveals his character through the Bible (vs. 7–11), and God allows us to experience his forgiveness through daily life (vs. 12–14).

Question 3: The group may wish to look up other verses that describe the results of obedience: Deuteronomy 6:3; John 15:10; Acts 5:32; Romans 2:13; 2 Corinthians 9:13, 14; Hebrews 5:8, 9.

Question 8: David offered praise to God for his many blessings. Ask group members to quietly meditate on the blessings they have received from God. Then spend time encouraging each other with stories of God's blessings and praising him for what he has done.

LESSON FOUR

Question 3: Sheep rely on the shepherd for everything: guidance, protection, all of their basic needs. In the same way, we follow the Good Shepherd and depend on him for our needs.

Question 9: Group members cannot apply the truth of this lesson until they understand what keeps them from turning to the Good Shepherd and enjoying the rest he offers. Challenge participants to identify ways they can experience God's rest more fully. The New Testament refers to Jesus as the Good Shepherd (John 10:11), the great Shepherd (Hebrews 13:20, 21), and the Head Shepherd (1 Peter 5:4).

LESSON FIVE

Psalm 32 expresses the joy and relief David felt when God forgave him for his sin with Bathsheba. Prepare yourself for this lesson by reading the story of David's adultery with Bathsheba and his murder of her husband Uriah (2 Samuel 11 and 12).

Question 2: Ask a group member to read aloud the story of David's attempts to cover up his sin with Bathsheba (2 Samuel 11:6–27). Emphasize the result of David's cover-up, and discuss the dangers of trying to hide our mistakes from God.

Question 4: Encourage participants to find the answer in these verses: Psalm 38:4, 22; 130:1–4; Micah 7:16–19; Hebrews 10:22.

Give the group an assignment for next week: Memorize 1 John 1:9.

LESSON SIX

Question 2: Some members of your group may be struggling to cope with their fears. Encourage them to turn to God for security and peace. Remind them that only God can help them overcome their fears.

Question 5: The Israelites set up physical landmarks to remind them of God's provision and protection (see Genesis 8:18 and Joshua 4:1–9; 24:26–27). The group may want to spend some time telling stories of how God has displayed his power in their lives. They will see firsthand that taking time to remember God's power in the past gives hope for the future.

LESSON SEVEN

David wrote this psalm after the prophet Nathan declared God's judgment against him because of his adultery with Bathsheba and his murder of her husband.

Question 4: David felt guilty about his affair with Bathsheba and tried to cover it up by murdering her husband, but he did not repent until Nathan revealed God's knowledge of his sin and judgment on him. Remind the group that we also need God's correction to bring us to repentance.

Question 7: These related passages may contribute to the group's discussion: Job 36:10; Proverbs 6:23; John 16:7, 8; 1 Thessalonians 1:4, 5; 2 Timothy 3:16.

LESSON EIGHT

David wrote this psalm during the time of his son's rebellion (2 Samuel 15–18). Even in the midst of this heartbreaking and seemingly hopeless situation, David knew God was in control. He found true relief and happiness because he put his hope in God.

Question 4: Believing in God does not exempt us from life's problems and pain. Instead, our faith in God gives us the courage and strength to face our trials. This psalm teaches us that the key to resolving problems is to depend on God for help and wisdom.

Question 5: Your group may want to learn more about what the Bible teaches about the value of power, wealth, and status. Refer them to these passages (either for independent study or future group study): Deuteronomy 8:18; Ecclesiastes 5:10; Luke 12:15; 14:7–14; Romans 12:16; 1 Timothy 6:17–19; James 1:9–11; 5:1–3.

LESSON NINE

Question 5: Give group members time to think through this question. These passages may contribute to the group's understanding of the fear of God: Exodus 3:5; Deuteronomy 10:12; Joshua 24:14; Psalm 89:7; Ecclesiastes 12:13; Isaiah 8:13; Habakkuk 2:20; Matthew 10:28; 1 Peter 1:17; 2:17.

Question 6: The frailty of life should not discourage or frighten us, it should motivate us to live well. Reminding ourselves that life is short should sharpen our focus and concentrate our efforts on what is important.

LESSON TEN

Question 2: Give the group a few moments to ponder what it means to praise God. Encourage them to think of new, creative ways to offer their praise to God. The group might want to set aside some time later in the meeting to put their ideas into practice.

Question 6: The group can learn more about God's mercy and compassion by reading these passages: 1 Chronicles 21:13; Nehemiah 9:17; Psalm 103:13; 145:9; Daniel 9:18; Luke 1:50; Romans 9:18; James 5:11; 1 Peter 1:3. If time permits, select several of these passages for participants to read aloud.

LESSON ELEVEN

Psalms 125 and 126 celebrate God's protection and power. God demonstrates his power by saving us from sin and restoring us to a right relationship with him.

Question 4: Other passages in the Bible talk about the triumph of good over evil. Look up Psalm 60:12; 118:7; 1 Corinthians 15:54-57; 2 Corinthians 2:14; 1 John 5:4, 5; Revelation 5:5.

Question 6: Read aloud Romans 10:9. One way your group can apply the truth of this lesson is to think of ways to share the good news of salvation with others. Ask each group member to write down the name of someone who has not experienced God's saving power. Pray together for wisdom and courage to share the gospel with those people.

LESSON TWELVE

Question 6: Challenge group members to take an objective look at their lifestyles to determine whether God is the head of their home. Ask this question: How is a God-ruled household different from a family who does not know God?

Question 7: Some people do not like talking about the problems Christian families face, but ignoring or glossing over our problems makes things worse. The Bible encourages believers to depend on each other for help, comfort, and encouragement. If a member of your group shares about a current family problem, take time to pray for him or her.

ADDITIONAL NOTES

ADDITIONAL NOTES

ADDITIONAL NOTES

ADDITIONAL NOTES

ADDITIONAL NOTES

ADDITIONAL NOTES

ADDITIONAL NOTES

ADDITIONAL NOTES

ACKNOWLEDGMENTS

Campolo, Tony. *It's Friday, But Sunday's Comin',* copyright 1984, Word, Inc., Dallas, Texas.

Graham, Billy. *How to Be Born Again*, copyright 1971, Word, Inc., Dallas, Texas.

Graham, Billy. *Storm Warning*, copyright 1992, Word Inc., Dallas, Texas.

Lucado, Max. *The Applause of Heaven*, copyright 1990, Word Inc., Dallas, Texas.

Lucado, Max. *God Came Near*, Questar Publishers, Multnomah Books, copyright 1987 by
   Max Lucado.

Lucado, Max. *No Wonder They Call Him the Savior*, Questar Publishers, Multnomah Books,
   copyright 1986 by Max Lucado.

Lucado, Max. *Six Hours One Friday*, Questar Publishers, Multnomah Books, copyright 1989 by
   Max Lucado.

Lucado, Max. *Tell Me the Story*, copyright 1992. Used by permission of Good News Publishers,
   Crossway Books, Wheaton, Illinois 60187.

Lucado, Max. *When God Whispers Your Name*, copyright 1994, Word Inc., Dallas, Texas.

Swindoll, Charles. *Living Above the Level of Mediocrity*, copyright 1987, Word, Inc., Dallas,
   Texas.

Swindoll, Charles. *Strengthening Your Grip*, copyright 1982, Word, Inc., Dallas, Texas.